MARTIN
STOREY'S

EASY

CABLE

KNITS

MARTIN
STOREY'S

EASY

CABLE

KNITS

10 designs with
a contemporary
twist

Photography by
Steven Wooster

BERRY&**CO**

Martin Storey's Easy Cable Knits

First published in 2017 by
Berry & Co (Publishing) Ltd
47 Crewys Road, London NW2 2AU
Copyright © Berry & Co (Publishing)
2017
www.berrypublishing.co.uk

Designs copyright © **Martin Storey**
2017

Design **Steven Wooster**
Pattern writing (and knitting) **Penny
Hill**, **Frances Jago** and **Martin Storey**
Pattern checking **Marilyn Wilson**
Charts **Anne Wilson**
Styling **Susan Berry**

British Library Cataloguing in
Publication Data
A catalogue record of this book is
available from the British Library.
ISBN 978-0-9927968-8-4

Printed in the United Kingdom

CONTENTS

INTRODUCTION

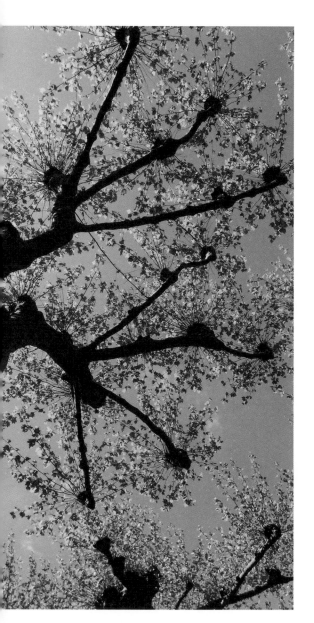

As those of you familiar with my knitwear designs will know, cables are my thing! In part because of their history in traditional Aran knitting patterns, but mostly because they create really interesting stitch texture in so many ways. You can play almost endlessly with the variations. But, and this is what surprises people, cables are not actually difficult to knit. You just need to understand the basic principle: which is that you are moving a set number of stitches across another set number of stitches in a repeating pattern of rows. Once you master the basics, the world, as they say, is your oyster! And if you need help with the basics, then you might find my little book, **Learn to Knit Cables**, published as a sister volume to this one, a help.

I created the 10 designs in this book primarily for people who have mastered the basics of knitting and are now ready to move into designs with more interesting stitches. To this end, I have created simple shaped garments with interesting cable panels or edgings, as well as cabled items without shaping, such as fingerless mittens, a cowl, a cushion and a throw. As the choice of yarn is so important to the way the cable texture looks, I have chosen Rowan Hemp Tweed which shows off the cables to best advantage.

The beautiful landscape of the Dordogne – a stone's throw from where the first cave paintings were discovered – seemed a wholly appropriate location for the knits in this book: luminous, light and natural, it had just the ambience we wanted for a collection of designs that are easy to knit, easy to wear and are timeless. And I am most grateful to the two young French students from Bordeaux university who modelled the garments for us with effortless style.

GALLERY

TENDRIL CABLE SCARF

Super-sized cables are perfect for a very simple, extra long scarf, which can be joined at each end so it can be worn looped several times around the neck, as shown here. This elongated plait design is both soft and stylish.

CHAIN CABLE SLIPOVER

This neat little slipover is perfect for layering over a printed dress or shirt. The staghorn cable panel on the front and back is bordered with a right and left twist cable on either side.

CORKSCREW CABLE SHAWL

This has just a hint of a cable forming the straight edge of the triangular shawl and then continuing to form a long tail that can be knotted or looped around, with a fringe at each end.

CABLE EDGE JACKET

This is another simply constructed garment with drop shoulders and a boxy
shape; the cuffs of the short sleeves and the front bands are each decorated
with the same simple cable. It can be worn dressed up or dressed down,
with jeans (see page 33).

WOODLAND CABLE BLANKET

It is fun to have a simple patched project on the go. This pretty little blanket has an alternating lacy tree and leaf design for each of the patches, and the assembled blanket is trimmed with a rope cable edging.§

GARTER TWIST COWL

A cowl is a great first-time cable project, as it has no shaping. The same alternating stocking stitch and garter stitch cable pattern repeats around the cowl, with a deep rib at the top and bottom.

LINKS CABLE CARDIGAN

A classic V-neck, longer length cardigan is made special with a cable panel bordering the button band on the left and right fronts.

MOSS TWIST MITTENS

This is another great introductory cable knit project with its interesting textural stitch variation to the simple cable panel on the back of the fingerless mittens.

WAVE CABLE CARDIGAN

The narrow cable panel on this elegant short cardigan is simple but very effective.
The cardigan design is enhanced by the garter-stitch yoke front and back, and
the simple rolled garter-stitch collar.

WINDOWPANE CUSHION

This small moss-stitch and simple repeating cable design is
used for two identical cushions in toning colourways. The
back of each cushion is moss-stitch only.

PATTERNS

CABLE EDGE JACKET

YARN
12(13:15:16) x 50g balls Rowan Hemp Duck Egg 139

NEEDLES
Pair each 4mm (US 6) and 4.5mm (US 7) knitting needles. Circular 4mm (US 6) and 4.5mm (US 7) knitting needles. Cable needle.

32

TENSION
19 sts and 25 rows to 10cm/4in square over st st using 4.5mm (US 7) needles or size to obtain correct tension.

ABBREVIATIONS
C8B Slip next 4 sts on to a cable needle, hold at back of work, k4, then k4 from cable needle.
C8F Slip next 4 sts on to a cable needle, hold at front of work, k4, then k4 from cable needle.
See also page 63.

To fit bust

92-97	102-107	112-117	122-127	cm
36-38	40-42	44-46	48-50	in

Finished measurements
Bust

128	140	152	165	cm
50½	55	60	66	in

Length to back neck

67	70	73	76	cm
26½	27½	28¾	30	in

BACK
With 4mm (US 6) circular needle, cast on 123(135:147:159) sts.
Work backwards and forwards in rows.
K 6 rows.
Change to 4.5mm (US 7) circular needle and patt
Row 1(RS) K to end.
Row 2 P to end.
Row 3 K3, [p1, k3] to end.
Row 4 P to end.
Row 5 K to end.
Row 6 P to end.
Row 7 K1, [p1, k3] to last 2 sts, p1, k1.
Row 8 P to end.
These 8 rows form the patt and are repeated throughout.
Cont in patt until back measures 35(36:37:38)cm/13¾(14:14½:15)in from cast-on edge ending with a WS row.
Armhole border
Row 1 Cast on 13 sts, k these 13 sts, then patt to end.
Row 2 Cast on 13 sts, k3, p7, k3, patt to last 13 sts, k3, p7, k3. *149(161:173:185) sts.*
Row 3 K13, patt to last 13 sts, k13.
Row 4 K3, p2, [m1, p1] 5 times, k3, patt to last 13 sts, k3, p2, [m1, p1] 5 times, k3. *159(171:183:195) sts.*
Cont in cable patt.
Row 1 Work Row 1 of Chart, patt to last 18 sts.
Row 2 Work Row 2 of Chart, patt to last 18 sts.
These 2 rows set the 12-row, 18-st cable panel at each end of the row.
Cont in patt until back measures 58(60:62:64)cm/23(23½:24½:25¼)in from cast-on edge ending with a right side row.
Next row K3, p2, [p2tog] 5 times, k3, patt to last 18 sts, k3, p2, [p2tog] 5 times, k3. *149(161:173:185) sts.*
Shape shoulder
Cast off 13 sts at beg of next 2 rows. *123(135:147:159) sts.*
Cast off 6 sts at beg of next 20(22:24:26) rows. *3 sts.*

Work 3tog and fasten off.

POCKET LININGS (both alike)
Using 4.5mm (US 7) needles cast on 30(34:34:38) sts.
Beg with a k row, work 30(32:34:36) rows in st st.
Leave these sts on a holder.

LEFT FRONT
With 4mm (US 6) needles cast on 72(78:84:90) sts.
K 6 rows.
Change to 4.5mm (US 7) needles and patt.
Row 1 (RS) K to end.
Row 2 K3, p2, [m1, p1] 5 times, k3, for cable border, p to end.
77(83:89:95) sts.
Row 3 K3(5:3:5), [p1, k3] to last 18 sts, k18.
Row 4 K3, p12, k3, p to end.
Row 5 K to last 18 sts, k3, C8B, k7.
Row 6 K3, p12, k3, p to end.
Row 7 K1(3:1:3), [p1, k3] to last 20 sts, p1, k19.
Row 8 K3, p12, k3, p to end.
These 8 rows form the main patt and the first 6 rows of the cable panel.
Work rows 7-12 from Chart, then repeat the 12 rows **at the same time** work a further 24(26:28:30) rows.

Place pocket
Next row Patt 16(18:24:26), place next 30(34:34:38) sts on a holder, patt across 30(34:34:38) sts of pocket lining, patt to end.
Cont in patt until front measures 35(36:37:38)cm/13¾(14:14½:15)in from cast-on edge ending with a wrong side row.

Armhole border
Row 1 Cast on 13 sts, k these 13 sts, then patt to end.
Row 2 Patt to last 13 sts, k3, p7, k3. *90(96:102:108) sts.*
Row 3 K13, patt to end.
Row 4 Patt to last 13 sts, k3, p2, [m1, p1] 5 times, k3. *95(101:107:113) sts.*
Cont in cable patt.
Row 1 Work Row 1 of Chart, patt to end.
Row 2 Patt to last 18 sts, work Row 2 of Chart.
These 2 rows set the cable panel for armhole border.
Cont in patt until front measures 58(60:62:64)cm/23(23½:24½:25¼)in from cast on edge ending with a right side row.
Next row Patt to last 18 sts, k3, p2, [p2tog] 5 times, k3. *90(96:102:108) sts.*

Shape shoulder
Next row Cast off 13 sts, patt to end. *77(83:89:95) sts.*
Patt 1 row.
Cast off 6 sts at beg of next and 9(10:11:12) foll right side rows. *17 sts.*
Next row K3, p2, [p2tog] 5 times, k2. *12 sts.*
Cast off.

KEY
☐ K on RS, P on WS
▣ P on RS, K on WS

C8B

C8F

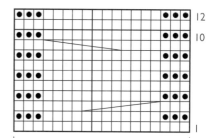

18 sts

RIGHT FRONT

With 4mm (US 6) needles cast on 72(78:84:90) sts.

K 6 rows.

Change to 4.5mm (US 7) needles and patt.

Row 1 (RS) K to end.

Row 2 P59(65:71:77), k3, p2, [m1, p1] 5 times, k3, for cable border. *77(83:89:95) sts.*

Row 3 K18, for border, [k3,p1] to last 3(5:3:5)sts, k3(5:3:5).

Row 4 P to last 18 sts, k3, p12, k3.

Row 5 K3, C8B, k to end.

Row 6 P to last 18 sts, k3, p12, k3.

Row 7 K19, p1, [k3, p1] to last 1(3:1:3)sts, k1(3:1:3).

Row 8 P to last 18 sts, k3, p12, k3.

These 8 rows form the main patt and the first 6 rows of the cable panel. Work rows 7-12 from Chart, then repeat the 12 rows at the same time work a further 24(26:28:30) rows.

Place pocket

Next row Patt 31, place next 30(34:34:38) sts on a holder, patt across 30(34:34:38) sts of pocket lining, patt to end.

Cont in patt until front measures 35(36:37:38)cm/13¾(14:14½:15)in from cast-on edge ending with a right side row.

Armhole border

Row 1 Cast on 13 sts, k3, p7, k3, patt to end. *90(96:102:108) sts.*

Row 2 Patt to last 13sts, k13.

Row 3 K3, p2, [m1, p1] 5 times, k3, patt to end. *95(101:107:113) sts.*

Cont in cable patt.

Row 1 Patt to last 18 sts, work Row 1 of Chart.

Row 2 Work Row 2 of Chart, patt to end.

These 2 rows set the cable panel for armhole border.

Cont in patt until front measures 58(60:62:64)cm/23(23½:24½:25¼)in from cast-on edge ending with a right side row.

Next row K3, p2, [p2tog] 5 times, k3, patt to end. *90(96:102:108) sts.*

Patt 1 row.

Shape shoulder

Next row Cast off 13 sts, patt to end. *77(83:89:95) sts.*

Patt 1 row.

Cast off 6 sts at beg of next and 8(9:10:11) foll wrong side rows. *17 sts.*

Patt 1 row.

Next row Cast off 6 sts, k next st, p2, [p2tog] 5 times, k3. *12 sts.*

Cast off.

POCKET TOPS (both alike)

With right side facing, using 4mm (US 6) needles, place sts on a needle.

Row 1 K4, [p2, k2] to last 6 sts, p2, k4.

Row 2 K2, [p2, k2] to end.

Rep the last 2 rows twice more.

Cast off in rib.

34

TO MAKE UP
Join shoulder seams. Join cast-off edges of front bands. Join side and cast-on edges of armbands. Sew down pocket linings and pocket tops.

SIZE
42cm/16½in at widest part.

YARN
7 x 50g balls of Rowan Hemp Tweed Kelp 142.

NEEDLES
Pair each 4mm (US 6) and 4.5mm (US 7) knitting needles.
Cable needle.

36

TENSION
19 sts and 34 rows to 10cm/4in square over st st using 4.5mm (US 7) needles or size to obtain correct tension.

ABBREVIATIONS
C8B Slip next 4 sts on a cable needle and leave at back of work, k4, then k4 from cable needle. See also page 63.

CORKSCREW CABLE SHAWL

TO MAKE
Using 4mm (US 6) needles cast on 11 sts.
Row 1 K1, [yf, k2tog] 5 times.
Row 2 Sl 1, k to end.
Rep the last row 4 times more.
Change to 4.5mm (US 7) needles.
Next row Sl 1, k to end.
Inc row Sl 1, k3, [p1, m1] 3 times, k4. *14 sts.*
Work in cable patt.
Row 1 Sl 1, k13.
Row 2 Sl 1, k2, p8, k3.
Rows 3 and 4 As rows 1 and 2.
Row 5 Sl 1, k2, C8B, k3.
Row 6 As row 2.
Rows 7 to 10 Rep rows 1 and 2 twice.
These 10 rows form the cable panel.
Work a further 80 rows, ending with a 10th row.
Shape side
Row 1 (RS) Sl 1, patt to end.
Row 2 Sl 1, patt to end.
Row 3 Sl 1, patt to end.
Row 4 Sl 1, k1, inc in next st, patt to end. *15 sts.*
Rows 5 to 296 Working inc sts into g-st, rep the last 4 rows 73 times. *88 sts.*
Row 297 (RS) Sl 1, patt to end.
Row 298 Sl 1, patt to end.
Row 299 Sl 1, patt to end.
Row 300 Sl 1, k1, k2tog, patt to end. *87 sts.*
Rows 301 to 592 Rep the last 4 rows 73 times. *14 sts.*
Work 89 rows in patt, ending row 1.
Next row Sl 1, k2, p1, [p2tog] 3 times, p1, k3. *11 sts.*
Change to 4mm (US 6) needles.
Next row Sl 1, k to end.
Rep the last row 5 times more.
Next row K1, [yf, k2tog] 5 times.
Cast off.

MAKE UP
Cut forty 60cm (24in) lengths of yarn. Knot 4 lengths through each eyelet at each end.

CHAIN CABLE SLIPOVER

YARN
6(7:7:8) × 50g balls of Rowan Hemp Tweed Almond 141.

NEEDLES
Pair each 3.75mm (US 5) and 4.5mm (US 7) knitting needles. Cable needle.

38

TENSION
20 sts and 25 rows to 10cm/4in square over moss st using 3.75mm (US 5) needles or size to obtain correct tension

ABBREVIATIONS
C4F Slip next 2 sts on to a cable needle and hold at front of work, k2, then k2 from cable needle.
C4B Slip next 2 stitches onto cable needle and hold at back of work, k2, then k2 from cable needle.
C6F Slip next 3 sts on to a cable needle and hold at front of work, k3, then k3 from cable needle.
C6B Slip next 3 stitches onto cable needle and hold at back of work, k3, then k3 from cable needle.
See also page 63.

To fit bust

82-86	92-97	102-107	112-117	cm
32-34	36-38	40-42	44-46	in

Finished measurements
Bust

88	100	112	124	cm
34¾	39½	44	48¾	in

Length to back neck

52	54	56	58	cm
20½	21¼	22	23¾	in

BACK
Using 3.75mm (US 5) needles cast on 98(110:122:134) sts.
Rib row 1 P2(0:2:0), [k2, p2] 8(10:11:13) times, k4, p2, [k2, p2] 5 times, k4, [p2, k2] 8(10:11:13) times, p2(0:2:0).
Rib row 2 K2(0:2:0), [p2, k2] 8 (10:11:13) times, p4, k2, [p2, k2] 5 times, p4, [k2, p2] 8(10:11:13) times, k2(0:2:0).
Rib row 3 P2(0:2:0), [k2, p2] 8(10:11:13) times, C4B, p2, [k2, p2] 5 times, C4F, [p2, k2] 8(10:11:13) times, p2(0:2:0).
Rib row 4 K2(0:2:0), [p2, k2] 8(10:11:13) times, p4, k2, [p2, k2] 5 times, p4, [k2, p2] 8(10:11:13) times, k2(0:2:0).
Rep these 4 rows once more.
Change to 4.5mm (US 7) needles and patt.
Row 1 [K1, p1] 16(19:22:25) times, p2, work across row 1 of cable panel, p2, [p1, k1] 16(19:22:25) times.
Row 2 [K1, p1] 16(19:22:25) times, k2, work across row 2 of cable panel, k2, [p1, k1] 16(19:22:25) times.
These 2 rows form the moss st and set the cable panel position.
Dec row Moss st to 3 sts before cable panel, p2tog, p1, work across cable panel, p1, p2tog, moss st to end.
Patt 5 rows as set.
Rep the last 6 rows 3 times more and the Dec row again.
Work 9 row straight.
Inc row Moss st to 2 sts before cable panel, m1, p2, work across cable panel, p2, m1, moss st to end.
Rep the last 10 rows 4 times more.
Cont in patt until work measures 31(32:33:34)cm/12¼(12½:13:13¼)in from cast-on edge, ending with a wrong side row.
Shape armholes
Cast off 7(9:11:13) sts at beg of next 2 rows. *84(92:100:108) sts.*
Next row Skpo, patt to last 2 sts, k2tog.
Next row Patt to end.
Rep the last 2 rows 6(7:8:9) times more. *70(76:82:88) sts ***.
Cont straight until Back measures 50(52:54:56)cm/19¾(20½:21¼:22)in from

cast-on edge, ending with a wrong side row.

Shape shoulders and back neck

Next row Patt 15(17:19:21), turn and work on these sts for first side of back neck.

Dec one st at neck edge on next 3 rows. *12(14:16:18) sts.*

Shape shoulder

Cast off.

With right side facing, place centre 40(42:44:46) sts on a spare needle, rejoin yarn to rem sts, patt to end.

Dec one st at neck edge on next 3 rows. *12(14:16:18) sts.*

Patt 1 row.

Shape shoulder

Cast off.

FRONT

Work as given for Back to **.

Shape front neck

Next row Patt 22(24:26:28) sts, turn and work on these sts for first side of neck shaping.

Dec one st at neck edge on every right side row until 12(14:16:18) sts rem.

Work straight until front measures the same as back to shoulder, ending at armhole edge.

Shape shoulder

Cast off.

With right side facing, place centre 26(28:30:32) sts on a spare needle, rejoin yarn to rem sts, patt to end.

Dec one st at neck edge on every right side row until 12(14:16:18) sts rem.

Work straight until front measures the same as back to shoulder, ending at armhole edge.

Patt 1 row.

Shape shoulder

Cast off.

NECKBAND

Join right shoulder seam.

With right side facing using 3.75mm (US 5) needles pick up and k32(34:36:38) sts down left side of front neck, decreasing 8 sts, patt 26(28:30:32) sts from front neck holder, pick up and k32(34:36:38) sts up right side of front neck, 3 sts down right side of back neck, decreasing 10 sts, patt 40(42:44:46) sts from back neck holder, pick up and k3 sts up left side of back neck. *118(126:134:142) sts.*

Rib row 1 K2, [p2, k2] to end.

Rib row 2 P2, [k2, p2] to end.

Rib row 3 K2, [p2, k2] to end.

Cast off in rib.

ARMBANDS

Join left shoulder and neckband seam.

With right side facing, using 3.75mm (US 5) needles, pick up and k98(102:106:110) sts evenly round armhole edge.

Work 3 rows rib as given for neckband.

Cast off in rib.

MAKE UP

Join side and armband seams.

KEY

☐ K on RS, P on WS
▣ P on RS, K on WS
C4B
C4F
C6B
C6F

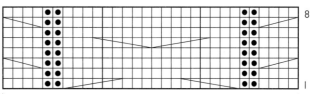

30 sts

GARTER TWIST COWL

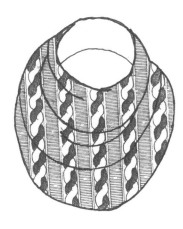

TO MAKE
Using 4mm (US 6) circular needle cast on 156 sts.
Taking care not to twist the sts, work in rounds.
Next round * [P2, k3] twice, [p2, k2] 4 times; rep from * 5 times.
Rep this round 9 times more.
Change to 4.5mm (US 7) circular needle and work in patt from Chart.
Round 1 [Work across Round 1 of 26-st patt rep] 6 times.
This round sets the 12-round patt repeat.
Work a further 59 rounds.
Next round * [P2, k3] twice, [p2, k2] 4 times; rep from * 5 times.
Rep this round 9 times more.
Cast off in rib.

SIZE
66cm/26in circumference;
28cm/11in deep.

YARN
3 x 50g balls of Rowan Hemp
Tweed Pumice 138.

NEEDLES
4mm (US 6) and 4.5mm (US 7)
circular knitting needles 60cm/24in
long.
Cable needle.

TENSION
19 sts and 25 rows to 10cm/4in
square over st st using 4.5mm
(US 7) needles or size to obtain
correct tension.

ABBREVIATIONS
C8B Slip next 4 sts on a cable
needle and leave at back of work,
k4, then k4 from cable needle.
See also page 63.

NOTE
When working from Chart all rows
are right side rows and read from
right to left.

KEY

☐ K on RS, P on WS

● P on RS, K on WS

⬜ C8B

26 sts

YARN
12(13:15:16) x 50g balls Rowan Hemp Tweed Kelp 142.

NEEDLES
Pair each 4mm (US 6) and 4.5mm (US 7) knitting needles.
Cable needle.

TENSION
19 sts and 25 rows to 10cm/4in square over st st using 4.5mm (US 7) needles or size to obtain correct tension.

EXTRAS
Six buttons

42

ABBREVIATIONS
C4F Slip next 2 sts on to a cable needle and hold at front of work, k2, then k2 from cable needle.
C4B Slip next 2 stitches onto cable needle and hold at back of work, k2, then k2 from cable needle.
C6F Slip next 3 sts on to a cable needle and hold at front of work, k3, then k3 from cable needle.
C6B Slip next 3 stitches onto cable needle and hold at back of work, k3, then k3 from cable needle.
See also page 63.

LINKS CABLE CARDIGAN

To fit bust

| 92-97 | 102-107 | 112-117 | 122-127 | cm |
| 36-38 | 40-42 | 44-46 | 48-50 | in |

Finished measurements
Bust

| 108 | 121 | 133 | 146 | cm |
| 42½ | 47¾ | 52½ | 57½ | in |

Length to Back neck

| 66 | 68 | 70 | 72 | cm |
| 26 | 26¾ | 27½ | 28½ | in |

Sleeve length
44cm/17¼in

BACK
With 4mm (US 6) needles cast on 105(117:129:141) sts.
Row 1 K1, [p1, k1] to end.
Row 2 P1, [k1, p1] to end.
These 2 rows form the rib.
Work a further 24 rows.
Change to 4.5mm (US 7) needles.
Beg with k row work in st st until back measures 63(65:67:69)cm/24¾ (25½:26½:27)in from cast-on edge, ending with a p row.
Shape upper arms
Cast off 7(8:9:10) sts at beg of next 6 rows. *63(69:75:81) sts.*
Shape shoulders
Cast off 13(14:15:16) sts at beg of next 2 rows.
Cast off rem 37(41:45:49) sts.

LEFT FRONT
With 4mm (US 6) needles cast on 58(64:70:76) sts.
Row 1 K1, [p1, k1] to last 3 sts, p1, k2.
Row 2 [K1, p1] to end.
These 2 rows form the rib.
Work a further 16 rows.
Change to 4.5mm (US 7) needles.
Row 1 K to last 31 sts, work across row 1 of Left front Chart, turn, cast on one st, leave rem 8 sts on a safety pin for front band. *51(57:63:69) sts.*
Row 2 P1, work across row 2 of Chart, p to end.
Row 3 K to last 24 sts, work across row 3 of Chart, k1.
These 3 rows set the Cable Panel with st st to the side.
Cont in patt until 66(70:74:78) rows fewer in st st have been worked than on Back to shape upper arms.
Neck shaping
Row 1 K to last 26 sts, k2tog, patt 24.
Patt 3 rows.

Left front

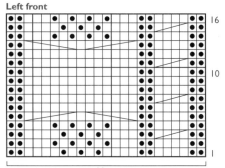

23 sts

Right front

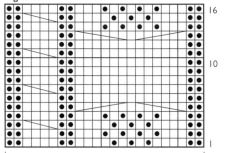

23 sts

KEY

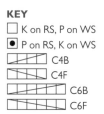

☐ K on RS, P on WS
⊙ P on RS, K on WS
C4B
C4F
C6B
C6F

Rep the last 4 rows 12(14:16:18) times and row 1 again. *37(41:45:49) sts.*
Work 13(9:5:1) rows straight.

Shape upper arm

Decreasing one st over 4-st cable and 2 sts over 13-st cable, cast off 7(8:9:10) sts at beg of next and 2 foll right side rows.
Work 1 row.

Shape shoulder

Cast off rem 13(14:15:16) sts.

RIGHT FRONT

With 4mm (US 6) needles cast on 58(64:70:76) sts.

Row 1 K2, [p1, k1] to end

Row 2 [P1, k1] to end.

These 2 rows form the rib.

Work a further 4 rows.

Buttonhole row Rib 3, skpo, yf, rib to end.

Work a further 11 rows.

Row 1 Rib 8, leave these sts on a safety pin for front band, then change to 4.5mm (US 7) needle, cast on 1 st, work across row 1 of Right front Chart, k to end. *51(57:63:69) sts.*

Cont with 4.5mm (US 7) needles.

Row 2 P to last 24 sts, work across row 2 of Chart, p1.

Row 3 K1, work across row 3 of Chart, k to end.

These 3 rows set the Cable Panel with st st to the side.

Cont in patt until 66(70:74:78) rows fewer have been worked than on Back to shape upper arms.

Neck shaping

Row 1 Patt 24, skpo, k to end.

Patt 3 rows.

Rep the last 4 rows 12(14:16:18) times and row 1 again. *37(41:45:49) sts.*

Work 14(10:6:2) rows straight.

Shape upper arm

Decreasing one st over 4-st cable and 2 sts over 13-st cable, cast off 7(8:9:10) sts at beg of next and 2 foll wrong side rows.

Work 1 row.

Shape shoulder

Cast off rem 13(14:15:16) sts.

LEFT FRONT BAND

With right side facing place sts on a 4mm (US 6) needle, inc in first st, rib to end. Cont in rib until band fits up left front and halfway across back neck. Cast off.

Mark position for buttons, the first on the 7th row of rib, the sixth 4 rows below beg of neck shaping and four spaced evenly between.

RIGHT FRONT BAND

With wrong side facing place sts on a 4mm (US 6) needle, inc in first st, rib to end.

Working buttonholes to match markers, cont in rib until band fits up right front and halfway across back neck. Cast off.

SLEEVES

With 4mm (US 6) needles cast on 45(49:53:57) sts.

Row 1 K1, [p1, k1] to end.

Row 2 P1, [k1, p1] to end.

These 2 rows form the rib.

Work a further 16 rows.

Change to 4.5mm (US 7) needles.

Beg with a k row, work in st st.

Inc row K4, m1, k to last 4 sts, m1, k4.

Work 3 rows.

Rep the last 4 rows 18 times and the inc row again. *85(89:93:97) sts.*

Cont straight until sleeve measures 44cm/17¼in from cast-on edge, ending with a wrong side row.

Shape top

Cast off 6 sts at beg of next 10 rows.

Cast off.

BUTTON BAND

Join right shoulder seam.

Cast off in rib.

TO MAKE UP

Join shoulder seams. Sew on front bands and join at centre back neck. With centre of sleeve to shoulder seam, sew on sleeves. Join side and sleeve seams. Sew on buttons.

MOSS TWIST MITTENS

RIGHT MITTEN

With 4mm (US 6) needles cast on 40 sts.

Rib row 1 [K2, p2] 6 times, k4, [k1, p1] twice, [p2, k2] twice.

Rib row 2 [P2, k2] twice, [p1, k1] twice, p4, [k2, p2] 6 times.

Rep these 2 rows twice.

Change to 4.5mm (US 7) needles.

Row 1 [K1, p1] 11 times, p2, slip next 4 sts on cable needle and hold at back of work, [k1, p1] twice, then k4 from cable needle, p2, [p1, k1] 3 times.

Row 2 [K1, p1] 3 times, k2, p4, [p1, k1] twice, k2, [p1, k1] 11 times.

Row 3 [K1, p1] 11 times, p2, [k1, p1] twice, k4, p2, [p1, k1] 3 times.

Row 4 [K1, p1] 3 times, k2, p4, [p1, k1] twice, k2, [p1, k1] 11 times.

Rows 5 to 10 Rep rows 3 and 4 three times.

Row 11 [K1, p1] 11 times, p2, slip next 4 sts on cable needle and hold at back of work, k4, then [k1, p1] twice, from cable needle, p2, [p1, k1] 3 times.

Row 12 [K1, p1] 3 times, k2, [p1, k1] twice, p4, k2, [p1, k1] 11 times.

Row 13 [K1, p1] 11 times, p2, k4, [k1, p1] twice, p2, [p1, k1] 3 times.

Row 14 [K1, p1] 3 times, k2, [p1, k1] twice, p4, k2, [p1, k1] 11 times.

Rows 15 to 20 Rep rows 13 and 14 three times.

** These 20 rows form the cable panel with moss st each side.

Work a further 40 rows, ending with a 20th row of patt.

Thumb shaping

Row 1 Inc in first st, patt to last 2 sts, inc in next st, moss st 1.

Row 2 Patt to end.

Rep the last 2 rows 7 times more. *56 sts.*

Next row Moss st 8, turn.

Work 6 rows in moss st.

Cast off in moss st.

Next row With right side facing, rejoin yarn to next st, patt to end.

Next row Moss st 8, turn.

Work 6 rows in moss st.

Cast off in moss st.

Next row With wrong side facing, rejoin yarn to next st, patt to end. *40 sts.*

Work a further 2 rows in patt, ending with a 20th row of patt.

Change to 4mm (US 6) needles.

Rib row 1 [K2, p2] 6 times, k4, [k1, p1] twice, [p2, k2] twice.

Rib row 2 [P2, k2] twice, [p1, k1] twice, p4, [k2, p2] 6 times.

Rep these 2 rows twice more.

Cast off in patt **.

LEFT MITTEN

With 4mm (US 6) needles cast on 40 sts.

Rib row 1 [K2, p2] twice, k4, [k1, p1] twice, [p2, k2] 6 times.

Rib row 2 [P2, k2] 6 times, [p1, k1] twice, p4, [k2, p2] twice.

Rep these 2 rows twice more.

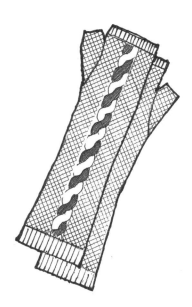

SIZE

To fit small/medium hands.
Length 29cm/11½in.

YARN

46

2 x 50g balls Rowan Hemp Tweed
Almond 141

NEEDLES

Pair each 4mm (US 6) and 4.5mm
(US 7) needles.
Cable needle.

TENSION

19 sts and 33 rows to 10cm (4in)
measured over moss st using
4.5mm (US 7) needles or size to
obtain correct tension.

ABBREVIATIONS

See also page 63.

Change to 4.5mm (US 7) needles.

Row 1 [K1, p1] 3 times, p2, slip next 4 sts on cable needle and hold at back of work, [k1, p1] twice, then k4 from cable needle, p2, [p1, k1] 11 times.

Row 2 [K1, p1] 11 times, k2, p4, [p1, k1] twice, k2, [p1, k1] 3 times.

Row 3 [K1, p1] 3 times, p2, [k1, p1] twice, k4, p2, [p1, k1] 11 times.

Row 4 [K1, p1] 11 times, k2, p4, [p1, k1] twice, k2, [p1, k1] 3 times.

Rows 5 to 10 Rep rows 3 and 4 three times.

Row 11 [K1, p1] 3 times, p2, slip next 4 sts on cable needle and hold at back of work, k4, then [k1, p1] twice, from cable needle, p2, [p1, k1] 11 times.

Row 12 [K1, p1] 11 times, k2, [p1, k1] twice, p4, k2, [p1, k1] 3 times.

Row 13 [K1, p1] 3 times, p2, k4, [k1, p1] twice,p2, [p1, k1] 11 times.

Row 14 [K1, p1] 11 times, k2, [p1, k1] twice, p4, k2, [p1, k1] 3 times.

Rows 15 to 20 Rep rows 13 and 14 three times.

Now work as given for Right Mitten from ** to **.

MAKE UP
Join side and thumb seams.

TENDRIL CABLE SCARF

BACK
Using 4.5mm (US 7) needles cast on 24 sts.
Rib row 1 P1, [k2, p2] five times, k2, p1.
Rib row 2 P3, [k2, p2] four times, k2, p3.
These 2 rows form the rib.
Work a further 29 rows.
Inc row P3, [m1, k2, m1, p2] 4 times, m1, k2, m1, p3. *34 sts.*
Work in Cable patt.
Row 1 P2, k30, p2.
Row 2 K2, p30, k2.
Rows 3 and 4 As Rows 1 and 2.
Row 5 P2, C20B, k10, p2.
Row 6 K2, p30, k2.
Rows 7 to 16 Rep Rows 1 and 2 five times.
Row 17 P2, k10, C20F, p2.
Row 18 K2, p30, k2.
Rows 19 to 24 Rep Rows 1 and 2 three times.
These 24 rows form the Cable patt.
Cont in Cable patt until scarf measures approx 238cm (94in) from cast-on edge, ending with Row 21.
Next row K2, [p2tog, p1] 10 times, k2. *24 sts.*
Work 31 rows in rib as given at beg.
Cast off in rib.

SIZE
Approx 9cm (3½in) wide; 250cm (98½in) long.

YARN
5 x 50g balls of Rowan Hemp Tweed Pine 135.

48

NEEDLES
Pair of 4.5mm (US 7) needles.
Cable needle.

TENSION
19 sts and 25 rows to 10cm/4in square over st st using 4.5mm (US 7) needles or size to obtain correct tension.

ABBREVIATIONS
C20F Slip next 10 sts on to a cable needle and hold at front of work, k10, then k10 from cable needle.
C20B Slip next 10 sts onto cable needle and hold at back of work, k10, then k10 from cable needle.
See also page 63.

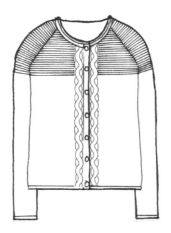

YARN
9(9:10:11:11:12) × 50g balls of
Rowan Hemp Tweed Cameo 140.

NEEDLES
Pair each 4mm (US 6) and 4.5mm
(US 7) knitting needles.
Cable needle.

TENSION
19 sts and 25 rows to 10cm/4in
square over st st using 4.5mm
(US 7) needles or size to obtain
correct tension.
19 sts and 34 rows to 10cm/4in
square over g-st using 4mm (US 6)
needles or size to obtain correct
tension.

50

EXTRAS
7 buttons

ABBREVIATIONS
C6F Slip next 3 sts on cable
needle and hold at front of work,
k3 then k3 from cable needle;
C6B Slip next 3 stitches on cable
needle and hold at back of work,
k3, then k3 from cable needle.
wrap 1 Slip stitch from left to right
needle purlwise, bringing yarn to
front, place slipped stitch back on
left needle.
See also page 63.

WAVE CABLE CARDIGAN

To fit bust

82	86	92	97	102	107	cm
32	34	36	38	40	42	in

Finished measurements
Bust

86	91	96	101	107	112	cm
34	35¾	37¾	39¾	42	44	in

Length to shoulder

53	54	55	56	58	59	cm
21	21¼	21¾	22	22¾	23¼	in

Sleeve length - all sizes
45cm (17¾in)

BACK
With 4mm (US 6) needles cast on 83(88:93:98:103:108) sts.
K 7 rows.
Change to 4.5mm (US 7) needles.
Beg with a k row, cont in st st until back measures 29(29:30:30:31:31)cm/
11½(11½:11¾:11¾:12¼:12¼)in from cast-on edge, ending with a p row.
Shape raglan armholes
Cast off 4(5:6:7:8:9) sts at beg of next 2 rows. *75(78:81:84:87:90) sts.*
Next row K2, skpo, k to last 4 sts, k2 tog, k2.
Next row P to end.
Rep the last 2 rows 6(7:8:9:10:11) times more. *61(62:63:64:65:66) sts.*
Change to 4mm (US 6) needles.
Next row K2, skpo, k to last 4 sts, k2 tog, k2.
K 3 rows.
Rep the last 4 rows 14 times. *31(32:33:34:35:36) sts.*
Leave these sts on a spare needle.

LEFT FRONT
With 4mm (US 6) needles cast on 45(48:50:53:56:58) sts.
Row 1 (WS) K7, p6, k to end.
Row 2 K to last 15 sts, p2, k6, p2, k5.
Row 3 K7, p6, k to end.
Row 4 K to last 15 sts, p2, C6B, p2, k5.
Row 5 K7, p6, k to end.
Rows 6 and 7 As rows 2 and 3.
Change to 4.5mm (US 7) needles.
Work in patt from Left front Chart.
Row 1 K to last 15 sts, p2, k6, p2 from Chart, k5.
Row 2 K5, then k2, p6, k2 from Chart, p to end.
These 2 rows set the 12-row cable panel and g-st front border with
st st body.
Work straight until front measures 29(29:30:30:31:31cm/

11½(11½:11¾:11¾:12¼:12¼)in from cast-on edge, ending with a wrong side row.

Shape raglan armhole

Next row Cast off 4(5:6:7:8:9) sts, patt to end. *41(43:44:46:48:49) sts.*

Next row Patt to end.

Next row K2, skpo, patt to end.

Next row Patt to end.

Rep the last 2 rows 6(7:8:9:10:11) times more. *34(35:35:36:37:37) sts.*

Change to 4mm (US 6) needles.

Next row K5(6:6:7:8:8), skpo, patt to end.

Patt 3 rows.

Rep the last 4 rows seven times. *26(27:27:28:29:29) sts.*

Shape front neck

Next row K5(6:6:7:8:8), skpo, k4, turn and leave remaining 15 sts on a holder.

K 3 rows.

Next row K5(6:6:7:8:8), skpo, k1, skpo.

K 3 rows.

Next row K5(6:6:7:8:8), skpo, k1.

K 3 rows.

Next row K5(6:6:7:8:8), skpo.

K 3 rows. *6(7:7:8:9:9) sts.*

Leave these sts on a spare needle.

Mark position for 7 buttons, the first on the 6th row, the seventh 2 rows below last row and the remaining five spaced evenly between.

RIGHT FRONT

With 4mm (US 6) needles cast on 45(48:50:53:56:58) sts.

Row 1 (WS) K to last 13 sts, p6, k7.

Row 2 K5, p2, k6, p2, k to end.

Row 3 K to last 13 sts, p6, k7.

Row 4 K5, p2, C6F, p2, k to end

Row 5 K to last 13 sts, p6, k7.

Row 6 (buttonhole row) K2, k2tog, yf, k1, p2, k6, p2, k to end

Row 7 K to last 13 sts, p6, k7.

Change to 4.5mm (US 7) needles.

Work in patt from Right front Chart.

Row 1 K5, then p2, k6, p2 from Chart, k to end.

Row 2 P to last 15 sts, k2, p6, k2 from Chart, then k5.

These 2 rows set the 12-row cable panel and g-st front border with st st body.

Working buttonholes to match markers, cont straight until front measures 29(29:30:30:31:31)cm/11½(11½:11¾:11¾:12¼:12¼)in from cast-on edge, ending with a right side row.

Shape raglan armhole

Next row Cast off 4(5:6:7:8:9) sts, patt to end. *41(43:44:46:48:49) sts.*

Next row Patt to last 4 sts, k2tog, k2.

Next row Patt to end.

Left front

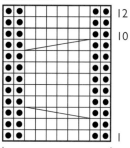

10 sts

Right front

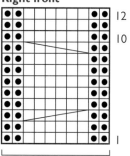

10 sts

KEY

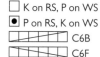

□ K on RS, P on WS

⬤ P on RS, K on WS

C6B

C6F

Rep the last 2 rows 6(7:8:9:10:11) times more. *34(35:35:36:37:37) sts.*
Change to 4mm (US 6) needles.
Next row Patt to last 7(8:8:9:10:10) sts, k2tog, k5(6:6:7:8:8).
Patt 3 rows.
Rep the last 4 rows 7 times. *26(27:27:28:29:29) sts.*

Shape front neck
Row 1 Decreasing 3 sts over cable, patt 15 sts, leave these 12 sts on a
holder, k4, k2tog, k5(6:6:7:8:8).
K 3 rows.
Next row K2tog, k1, k2tog, k5(6:6:7:8:8).
K 3 rows.
Next row K1, k2tog, k5(6:6:7:8:8).
K 3 rows.
Next row K2tog, k5(6:6:7:8:8).
K 3 rows. *6(7:7:8:9:9) sts.*
Leave these sts on a spare needle.

SLEEVES
With 4mm (US 6) needles cast on 38(42:46:50:54:58) sts.
K 7 rows.
Change to 4.5mm (US 7) needles.
Beg with a k row cont in st st.
Work 6 rows.
Inc row K3, m1, k to last 3 sts, m1, k3.
Work 7 rows.
Rep the last 8 rows 10 times and the inc row again. *62(66:70:74:78:82) sts.*
Cont straight until Sleeve measures 45cm/17¾in from cast-on edge, ending
with a wrong side row.

Shape raglan sleeve top
Cast off 4(5:6:7:8:9) sts at beg of next 2 rows. *54(56:58:60:62:64) sts.*
Next row K2, skpo, k to last 4 sts, k2 tog, k2.
Next row P to end.
Rep the last 2 rows 6(7:8:9:10:11) times more. *40 sts.*
Change to 4mm (US 6) needles.
Next row K2, skpo, k to last 4 sts, k2 tog, k2.
K 3 rows.
Rep the last 4 rows 11 times. *16 sts*

Left sleeve only
Shape top
Row 1 K2, skpo, k to last 2 sts, wrap 1, turn.
Row 2 K to end.
Row 3 K to last 3 sts, wrap 1, turn.
Row 4 K to end.
Row 5 K2, skpo, k to last 4 sts, wrap 1, turn.
Row 6 K to end.
Row 7 K to last 5 sts, wrap 1, turn.
Row 8 K to end.
Row 9 K2, skpo, k to last 6 sts, wrap 1, turn.

Row 10 K to end.
Row 11 K to last 7 sts, wrap 1, turn.
Row 12 K to end. *13 sts*
Leave these sts on a holder.
Right sleeve only
Shape top
Row 1 K to last 4 sts, k2 tog, k2.
Row 2 K to last 2 sts, wrap 1, turn.
Row 3 K to end.
Row 4 K to last 3 sts, wrap 1, turn.
Row 5 K to last 4 sts, k2 tog, k2.
Row 6 K to last 4 sts, wrap 1, turn.
Row 7 K to end.
Row 8 K to last 5 sts, wrap 1, turn.
Row 9 K to last 4 sts, k2 tog, k2.
Row 10 K to last 6 sts, wrap 1, turn.
Row 11 K to end.
Row 12 K to last 7 sts, wrap 1, turn. *13 sts*
Leave these sts on a holder.

NECKBAND
Join raglan seams.
With right side facing, using 4mm (US 6) needles place 12 sts from right
front on needle, pick up and k8 sts up right side of front neck, k6(7:7:8:9:9)
sts, k13 sts from right sleeve, 31(32:33:34:35:36) sts from back, 13 sts from
left sleeve, k6(7:7:8:9:9) sts, pick up and k8 sts down left side of front neck,
dec 3 sts over cable, k12 from left front holder.
Next row P10, p2tog, [p2, p2tog] 4 times, p to last 28 sts, p2tog, [p2, p2tog]
four times, p10.
Beg with a k row, work 4 rows in st st.
Cast off.

TO MAKE UP
Join side and sleeve seams. Sew on buttons.

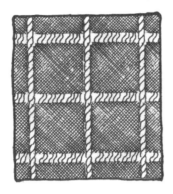

FRONT

Using 4.5 mm (US 7) needles cast on 60 sts.

Next row [RS] P1, [k1, p1] 3 times * [knit into front and back of next stitch] twice, [k1, p1] 10 times; rep from * once more, [knit into front and back of next stitch] twice, [k1, p1] 3 times, k1. *66 sts.*

Next row K1, [p1, k1] 3 times, p4, *[p1, k1] 10 times, p4; rep from * once more, [p1, k1] 3 times, p1.

Work in patt from Chart.

Row 1 [RS] P1, [k1, p1] 3 times * C4B, [k1, p1] 10 times [ie. the 24-st patt rep]; rep from * once more, C4B, [k1, p1] 3 times, k1.

Row 2 K1, [p1, k1] 3 times p4 * [p1, k1] 10 times, p4 [ie. the 24-st patt rep]; rep from * once more, [p1, k1] 3 times, p1.

SIZE

Cushion measures approx 30cm x 30cm (12in x 12in)

YARN

Cushion 1
3 x 50g balls Hemp Tweed Duck Egg 139
Cushion 2
3 x 50g balls Rowan Hemp Tweed Misty 137

NEEDLES

1 pair 4.5 mm (US 7) knitting needles
Cable needle

54

TENSION

19 sts and 32 rows to 10 cm (4in) square over moss stitch using 4.5mm (US 7) knitting needles or size to obtain correct tension.

EXTRAS

30 cm (12in) square cushion pad

ABBREVIATIONS

C4B Slip next 2 sts on to a cable needle and hold in back of work, k2, then k2 from cable needle.

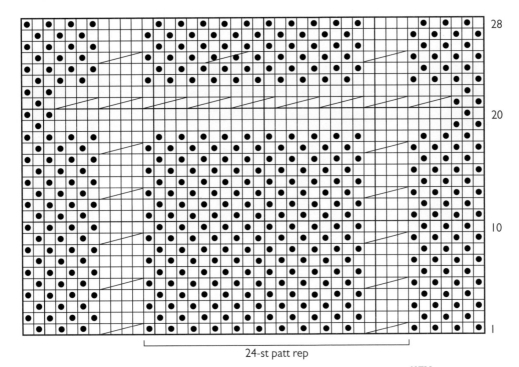

24-st patt rep

KEY
☐ K on RS, P on WS
⬛ P on RS, K on WS
▱▱ C4B

These 2 rows set the chart and 24-st repeat for the 28-row patt repeat.
Cont in patt to end of row 28.
Rep rows 1 to 28 from chart twice more, then work rows 1 to 13.
99 rows have been worked in total (WS facing for next row).
Row 100 [WS] K1, [p1, k1] 3 times, [p2tog] twice, *[p1, k1]
10 times, [p2tog] twice; rep from * once more, [p1, k1] 3 times,
p1. *60 sts.*
Cast off.

BACK
Using 4.5mm (US 7) needles cast on 59 sts.
Row 1 [RS] K1 * p1, k1; rep from * to end.
Row 2 As Row 1.
These 2 rows form the moss stitch patt.
Repeat these 2 rows until 100 rows have been worked in total
with RS facing for next row.
Cast off.

MAKE UP
With RS together, sew front and back along 3 sides. Insert
cushion pad. Join rem seam.

WOODLAND CABLE BLANKET

This throw is made like a patchwork from 35 squares to which the tree and leaf motifs are added and the squares then joined to make the throw, to which a separate cabled edging is added.

SIZE

Blanket measures approx 75cm x 105cm (29½in x 41½in) excluding cable trim

YARN

Rowan Hemp Tweed 50g balls:
A Almond 141 x 6
B Cameo 140 x 5
C Duck Egg 139 x 1
D Misty 137 x 2
E Treacle 134 x1
F Kelp 142 x 3
G Pumice 138 x 1
H Pine 135 x1

NEEDLES

1 pair 4.5 mm (US 7) knitting needles plus 1 spare 4.5mm (US 7) knitting needle
Cable needle

56

TENSION

19 sts and 25 rows to 10 cm (4in) square over st st using 4.5mm (US 7) needles or size to obtain correct tension.

ABBREVIATIONS

C4B Slip next 2 sts on to a cable needle and hold in back of work, k2 then k2 from cable needle.
C9B Slip next 4 sts on to a cable needle and hold in back of work, k5, then k4 from cable needle.

SQUARES
Make 35

Using 4.5mm (US 7) needles and A, cast on 30 sts.
Row 1 (RS) Sl1k, k to end.
Row 2 As Row 1.
Row 3 Sl1k, k to end.
Row 4 Sl1k, k1, P to last 2 sts, k2.
Rep Rows 3 and 4 until 39 rows have been worked in total with WS facing for next row.
Row 40 (WS) Sl1k, K to end.
Row 41 As row 40.
Next row (WS) Cast off knitwise.
Make a further 17 squares in A (18 in total).
Make 17 squares in B.

TREE MOTIF

Make 17.

Trunk

Using 4.5mm (US 7) needles and C, cast on 8 sts.
Row 1 (RS) P2, k4, p2.
Row 2 K2 p4, k2.
Row 3 P2, C4B, p2.
Row 4 As Row 2.
Rep these 4 rows once more, then Rows 1 to 3 inclusive, WS facing for next row.
Row 12 (WS) Ssk, p1, p2tog, p1, k2tog. *5 sts ***
With RS facing, leave these 5 sts on a spare needle.

Tree

Using 4.5mm (US 7) needles cast on 17 sts with C.
Row 1(RS) K6, with RS facing place trunk sts on spare needle behind main [left hand] needle and k2tog (the first stitch from main needle and trunk); rep for the next 4 trunk sts; then k6 the remaining sts on main [left hand] needle. Trunk now grafted on.
Row 2 Purl.
Row 3 Ssk, yf, ssk, K to last 4 sts, k2tog, yf, k2tog. *15 sts.*
Row 4 Purl.
Cont to rep Rows 3 and 4, 4 more times. *7 sts.*
Row 13 (RS) Ssk, yf, sl2K, k1, p2sso, yf, k2tog. *5 sts.*
Row 14 Purl.
Row 15 Ssk, k1, k2tog. *3 sts.*
Row 16 Purl.

Row 17 Sl2k, k1, p2sso. *1 st.*

Fasten-off.

Make a further 3 trees in C (4 in total).

Make 4 trees in A.

Make 6 trees in D.

Make 3 trees in E.

LEAF MOTIF

Make 18.

Using 4.5mm (US 7) needles and F cast on 8 sts.

Work trunk as given for Tree Motif to *** 5sts on needles.

Cont to work Leaf part as follows:

Row 1 (RS) Knit into front and back of first stitch, k1, yf, k1, yf, k1, k into front and back of last stitch. *9 sts.*

Row 2 Purl

Row 3 K4, yf, k1, yf, k4. *11 sts.*

Row 4 Purl

Row 5 K5, yf, k1, yf, k5. *13 sts.*

Row 6 Purl.

Row 7 Cast off 3 sts [1 st on right hand needle], k2, yf, k1, yf, k6. *12 sts.*

Row 8 Cast off 3 sts [1 st on right hand needle], p8. *9 sts.*

Rows 9 to 12 As Rows 3 to 6. *13sts.*

Row 13 Cast off 3 sts [1 st on right hand needle], k9. *10 sts*

Row 14 Cast off 3 sts [1 st stitch on right hand needle], p6. *7 sts.*

Row 15 Ssk, k3, k2tog. *5sts.*

Row 16 Purl.

Row 17 Ssk, k1, k2tog. *3 sts.*

Row 18 Purl.

Row 19 Sl1K, k2tog, psso. *1 st.*

Fasten-off

Make a further 5 leaves in F [6 in total].

Make 4 leaves in B.

Make 6 leaves in G.

Make 2 leaves in H.

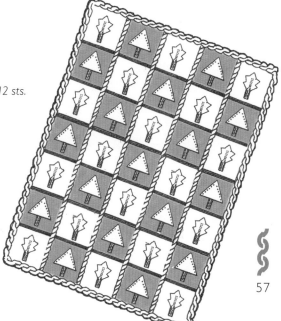

57

MAKE UP

Lightly block, steam and press all squares and motifs; each finished square should measure approx 15cm x 15cm (6in x 6in).

Placing motifs neatly and centrally on each square, so that the edges of the trunks run parallel with the rows of knitting, cont as folls:

Sew all Tree motifs to the B yarn squares (the darker coloured squares).

Sew all Leaf motifs to the A yarn squares (the lighter coloured squares).

Using a mattress or slip stitch, join all the squares together as shown in the sketch right. The squares should form a checkerboard pattern, with a lighter (A yarn) square in each of the four corners.

Cable Trim

Using 4.5mm (US 7) needles and F, cast on 11 sts.

Row 1 (RS) P2, k9.

Row 2 P9, k2.

Rows 3 and 4 As Rows 1 and 2.

Row 5 P2, C9B.

Row 6 As Row 2.

Rows 7 to 12 As Rows 1 and 2, three times.

These 12 rows form the patt.

Cont in patt until trim fits around entire edge of joined blanket squares, placing cabled edge at outer edge, and gathering trim at corners so it remains flat, ending with RS facing for next row.

Cast off.

Join ends of trim, then slip stitch trim in place.

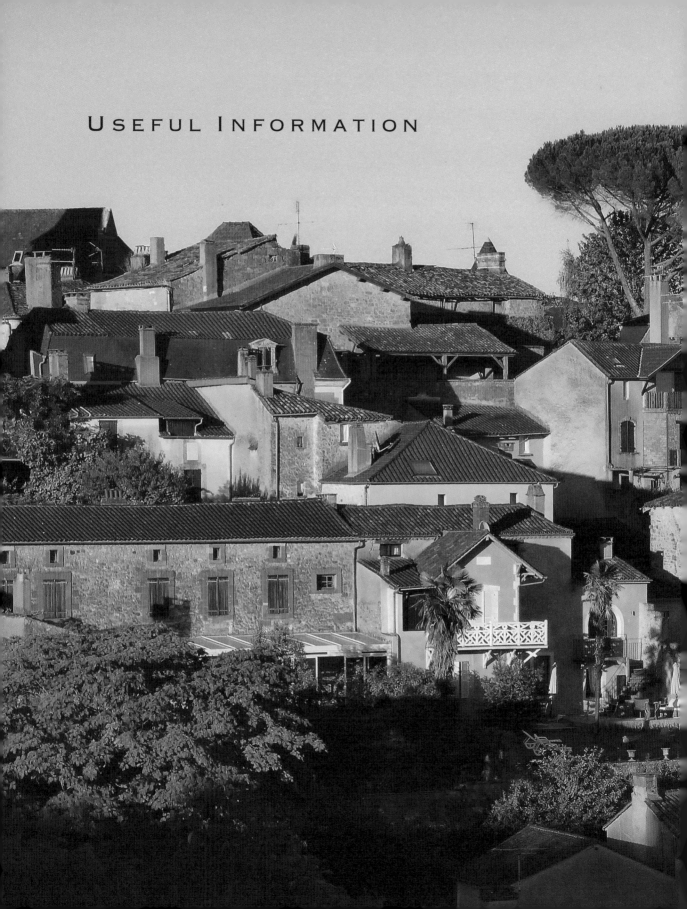

USEFUL INFORMATION

USEFUL INFORMATION

TENSION

Tension controls both the shape and size of an article, so any variation, however slight, can distort the finished piece of knitting. To check your tension, knit a square in the pattern stitch and/or stocking stitch of perhaps 5–10 more stitches and 5–10 more rows than those given in the tension note. Press the finished square under a damp cloth and mark out the central 10cm/4in square with pins. If you have more stitches to 10cm/4in than the given tension, try again using thicker needles. If you have fewer stitches than the given tension, try again using finer needles. Once you have achieved the correct tension, your project will be knitted to the measurements given.

CABLE PATTERNS

Cable stitch patterns allow you to twist the stitches in various ways, to create decorative effects to give an interesting rope-like structure to the knitting. The cables can be thin and fine (just a couple of stitches wide) or big and chunky (up to 8 stitches or more). To work cables, you need to hold the appropriate number of stitches that form the cable twist (abbreviated in pattern as C) on a separate small cable needle, while you knit behind or in front of them. You then knit the stitches off the cable needle before continuing to knit the remaining stitches in the row. Depending on whether the cable needle is at the front or the back of the work, the cables will twist to the left or right but the principle remains the same. A four-stitch cable will be abbreviated as C4F or C4B, depending on whether the cable needle is held to the front or back of the work. Abbreviations for the variations of cable, cross and twisted stitches are given in each pattern.

FINISHING METHODS

Pressing

Block out each piece of knitting by pinning it on a board to the correct measurements in the pattern. Then lightly press it according to the ball band instructions, omitting any ribbed areas. Take special care to press the edges, as this makes sewing up easier and neater. If you cannot press the fabric, then cover the knitted fabric with a damp cloth and allow it to stand for a couple of hours. Darn in all ends neatly along the selvedge edge or a colour join.

Stitching seams

When you stitch the pieces together, remember to match any areas of colour and texture carefully where they meet. Using a special seam stitch, called mattress stitch, creates the neatest flattest seam. Once all the seams are complete, press the seams and hems. Lastly, sew on the buttons to correspond with the positions of the buttonholes.

YARNS

The following Rowan yarn has been used in this book:
Rowan Hemp Tweed a blend of 75 per cent wool and 25 per cent hemp. Hemp fibre is resistant to stretching so does not distort with use and naturally softens with wear. 50g balls; 95m/104yd per ball; 19sts and 25 rows to 10cm/4in square using 4.5mm (US size 7) needles.

Abbreviations

alt	alternate	sk2po	sl 1, knit 2 together, pass slipped stitch over
approx	approximately	sl 1	slip one st
beg	begin(s)(ning)	sl1k	Slip one stitch knitwise
cm	centimetres		(with yarn in back of
cont	continu(e)(ing)		work)
dec	decreas(e)(ing)	sl2k	Slip two sts knitwise
foll(s)	follow(s)(ing)	ssk	Slip next 2 sts singly
g	gram		to RH needle knitwise,
g-st	garter stitch		insert tip of LH needle
in	inch(es)		through front loops of
inc	increas(e)(ing)		both sts and k together.
k	knit	st(s)	stitch(es)
k2tog	knit next 2 sts together	St st	stocking stitch (1 row k,
k3tog	knit next 3 sts together		1 row purl)
mm	millimetres	tbl	through back of loop(s)
M1	make one st by picking	tog	together
	up horizontal loop	WS	wrong side
	before next st and	yd	yard(s)
	knitting into back of it	yf	yarn forward
patt	pattern	yo	yarn over
p	purl	ytf	with yarn to front
psso	pass slipped stitch over	ytb	with yarn to back
p2tog	purl next 2 sts together	[ ]/*	repeat instructions
rem	remain(s)(ing)		within square brackets
rep	repeat		or between asterisk
RS	right side		
skpo	sl 1, k1, pass slipped stitch over		

Acknowledgments

A big, big thank you to the following: Steven and Susan for the wonderful photography, art direction, styling and graphics; Frances Jago for the beautifully knitted swatches and projects; Marilyn Wilson for her diligent checking; Ed for his diagrams; Laure Gautier and Juliette Rebiere-Olleans for modelling for us with such aplomb; and, of course, to the entire team at Rowan for their continuing support.

63

STOCKISTS

AUSTRALIA Australian Country Spinners, Pty Ltd, Level 7, 409 St. Kilda Road, Melbourne Vic 3004. **tel** 03 9380 3888 **fax** 03 9820 0989 **email** customerservice@auspinners.com.au

AUSTRIA MEZ Harlander GmbH, Schulhof 6, 1. Stock, 1010 Wien, Austria **tel** + 00800 26 27 28 00 **fax** (00) 49 7644 802-133 **email** verkauf.harlander@mezcrafts.com

BELGIUM MEZ crafts Belgium NV, c/o MEZ GmbH, Kaiserstr.1, 79341 Kenzingen, Germany **tel** 0032 (0) 800 77 89 2 **fax** 00 49 7644 802 133 **email** sales.be-nl@mezcrafts.com

BULGARIA MEZ Crafts Bulgaria EOOD, 7 Magnaurska Shkola Str, BG-1784 Sofia, Bulgaria **tel** (+359 2) 976 77 41 **fax** (+359 2) 976 77 20 **email** office.bg@mezcrafts.com

CANADA Sirdar USA Inc. 406 20th Street SE, Hickory, North Carolina, USA 28602 **tel** 828 404 3705 **fax** 828 404 3707 **email** sirdarusa@sirdar.co.uk

CHINA Commercial agent Mr Victor Li, c/o MEZ GmbH Germany, Kaiserstr. 1, 79341 Kenzingen / Germany **tel** (86-21) 13816681825 **email** victor.li@mezcrafts.com

CHINA SHANGHAI YUJUN CO.,LTD., Room 701 Wangjiao Plaza, No.175 Yan'an (E), 200002 Shanghai, China **tel** +86 2163739785 **email** jessechang@vip.163.com

CYPRUS MEZ Crafts Bulgaria EOOD, 7 Magnaurska Shkola Str., BG-1784 Sofia, Bulgaria **tel** (+359 2) 976 77 41 **fax** (+359 2) 976 77 20 **email** marketing.cy@mezcrafts.com

CZECH REPUBLIC Coats Czecho s.r.o.Staré Mesto 246 569 32 **tel** (420) 461616633 **email** galanterie@coats.com

DENMARK Carl J. Permin A/S Egegaardsvej 28 DK-2610 Rødovre **tel** (45) 36 72 12 00 **email** permin@permin.dk

ESTONIA MEZ Crafts Estonia OÜ, Ampri tee 9/4, 74001 Viimsi Harjumaa **tel** +372 630 6252 **email** info.ee@mezcrafts.com

FINLAND Prym Consumer Finland Oy, Huhtimontie 6, 04200 KERAVA **tel** +358 9 274871

FRANCE 3bcom, 35 avenue de Larrieu, 31094 Toulouse cedex 01, France **tel** 0033 (0) 562 202 096 **email** Commercial@3b-com.com

GERMANY MEZ GmbH, Kaiserstr. 1, 79341 Kenzingen, Germany **tel** 0049 7644 802 222 **email** kenzingen.vertrieb@mezcrafts.com **fax** 0049 7644 802 300

GREECE MEZ Crafts Bulgaria EOOD, 7 Magnaurska Shkola Str., BG-1784 Sofia, Bulgaria **tel** (+359 2) 976 77 41 **fax** (+359 2) 976 77 20 **email** marketing.gr@mezcrafts.com

HOLLAND G. Brouwer & Zn B.V., Oudhuijzerweg 69, 3648 AB Wilnis, Netherlands **tel** 0031 (0) 297-281 557 **email** info@gbrouwer.nl

HONG KONG East Unity Company Ltd, Unit B2, 7/F., Block B, Kailey Industrial Centre, 12 Fung Yip Street, Chai Wan **tel** (852)2869 7110 **email** eastunityco@yahoo.com.hk

ICELAND Carl J. Permin A/S Egegaardsvej 28 DK-2610 Rødovre **tel** (45) 36 72 12 00 **email** permin@permin.dk

ITALY Mez Cucirini Italy Srl, Viale Sarca, 223, 20126 MILANO **tel** 0039 0264109080 **email** servizio.clienti@mezcrafts.com **fax** 02 64109080

JAPAN Hobbyra Hobbyre Corporation, 23-37, 5-Chome, Higashi-Ohi, Shinagawa-Ku, 1400011 Tokyo. **tel** +81334721104 Daidoh International, 3-8-11 Kudanminami Chiyodaku, Hiei Kudan Bldg 5F, 1018619 Tokyo **tel** +81-3-3222-7076 **fax** +81-3-3222-7066

KOREA My Knit Studio, 3F, 144 Gwanhun-Dong, 110-300 Jongno-Gu, Seoul **tel** 82-2-722-0006 **email** myknit@myknit.com

LATVIA Coats Latvija SIA, Mukusalas str. 41 b, Riga LV-1004 **tel** +371 67 625173 **fax** +371 67 892758 **email** info.latvia@coats.com

LEBANON y.knot, Saifi Village, Mkhalissiya Street 162, Beirut **tel** (961) 1 992211 **fax** (961) 1 315553 **email** y.knot@cyberia.net.lb

LITHUANIA MEZ Crafts Lithuania UAB, A. Juozapaviciaus str. 6/2, LT-09310 Vilnius **tel** +370 527 30971 **fax** +370 527 2305 **email** info.lt@mezcrafts.com

LUXEMBOURG Coats N.V., c/o Coats GmbH, Kaiserstr.1, 79341 Kenzingen, Germany **tel** 00 49 7644 802 222 **fax** 00 49 7644 802 133 **email** sales.coatsninove@coats.com

MEXICO Estambres Crochet SA de CV, Aaron Saenz 1891-7Pte, 64650 MONTERREY **tel** +52 (81) 8335-3870 **email** abremer@redmundial.com.mx

NEW ZEALAND ACS New Zealand, P.O Box 76199, Northwood, Christchurch, New Zealand **tel** 64 3 323 6665 **fax** 64 3 323 6660 **email** lynn@impactmg.co.nz

NORWAY Carl J. Permin A/S Egegaardsvej 28 DK-2610 Rødovre **tel** (45) 36 72 12 00 **email** permin@permin.dk

PORTUGAL Mez Crafts Portugal, Lda – Av. Vasco da Gama, 774 - 4431-059 V.N. Gaia, Portugal **tel** 00 351 223 770700 **email** sales.iberia@mezcrafts.com

RUSSIA Family Hobby, 124683, Moskau, Zelenograd, Haus 1505, Raum III **tel** 007 (499) 270-32-47 Handtel. 007 916 213 74 04 **email** tv@fhobby.ru **web** www.family-hobby.ru

SINGAPORE Golden Dragon Store, BLK 203 Henderson Rd #07-02, 159546 Henderson Indurstrial Park Singapore **tel** (65) 62753517 **fax** (65) 62767112 **email** gdscraft@hotmail.com

SLOVAKIA MEZ Crafts Slovakia, s.r.o. Seberíniho 1, 821 03 Bratislava, Slovakia **tel** +421 2 32 30 31 19 **email** galanteria@mezcrafts.com

SOUTH AFRICA Arthur Bales LTD, 62 4th Avenue, Linden 2195 **tel** (27) 11 888 2401 **fax** (27) 11 782 6137 **email** arthurb@new.co.za

SPAIN MEZ Fabra Spain S.A, Avda Meridiana 350, pta 13 D, 08027 Barcelona **tel** +34 932908400 **fax** +34 932908409 **email** atencion.clientes@mezcrafts.com

SWEDEN Carl J. Permin A/S Egegaardsvej 28 DK-2610 Rødovre **tel** (45) 36 72 12 00 **email** permin@permin.dk

SWITZERLAND MEZ Crafts Switzerland GmbH, Stroppelstrasse20, 5417 Untersiggenthal, Switzerland **tel** +41 00800 2627 2800 **fax** 0049 7644 802 133 **email** verkauf.ch@mezcrafts.com

TURKEY MEZ Crafts Tekstil A.S, Kavacık Mahallesi, Ekinciler Cad. Necip Fazıl Sok. No.8 Kat: 5, 34810 Beykoz / Istanbul **tel** +90 216 425 88 10

TAIWAN Cactus Quality Co Ltd, 7FL-2, No. 140, Sec.2 Roosevelt Rd, Taipei, 10084 Taiwan, R.O.C. **tel** 00886-2-23656527 **fax** 886-2-23656503 **email** cqcl@ms17.hinet.net

THAILAND Global Wide Trading, 10 Lad Prao Soi 88, Bangkok 10310 **tel** 00 662 933 9019 **fax** 00 662 933 9110 **email** global.wide@yahoo.com

USA Sirdar USA Inc. 406 20th Street SE, Hickory, North Carolina, USA 28602 **tel** 828 404 3705 **fax** 828 404 3707 **email** sirdarusa@sirdar.co.uk

UK Mez Crafts U.K, 17F Brooke's Mill, Armitage Bridge, Huddersfield, HD4 7NR **web** www.mezcrafts.com**tel** 01484 950630

For more stockists in all countries please log on to **www.knitrowan.com**